Standing in Their Fire

Poems from a Hospital Nurse

Standing in Their Fire

Poems from a Hospital Nurse

by

Shawna L. Swetech, R.N.

© 2026 Shawna L. Swetech. All rights reserved.
This material may not be reproduced in any form,
published, reprinted, recorded, performed, broadcast,
rewritten, or redistributed without
the explicit permission of Shawna L. Swetech.
All such actions are strictly prohibited by law.

Cover design by Shay Culligan
Cover image by Shay Swetech, BFA
Author photo by Jay Swetech

ISBN: 978-1-63980-988-2
Library of Congress Control Number: 2025940814

Kelsay Books
502 South 1040 East, A-119
American Fork, Utah 84003
Kelsaybooks.com

This book is dedicated to
Jay Swetech for his love and encouragement,
to our children Mariah Giovanetti and Shay Swetech,
their spouses Nathanial Giovanetti and Jessica Ford-Helzer,
and to our granddaughters Lily and Zoë Helzer-Swetech.

And also, to my father L. Brooks Staton,
always my biggest fan,
who taped copies of my poems
to his refrigerator long into his old age.

Acknowledgments

I thank the editors of the following journals in which these poems appear or are forthcoming, sometimes in slightly different form:

American Journal of Nursing: "Cat-A-Tonic"
Ars Medica: "Rivulets of Rain"
The Healing Muse: "In Flames"
Marin Poetry Center Anthology: "Rituals"
Medicine and Meaning: "Rust"
Nursing2023: "In Their Fire," "Good Medicine"
The Permanente Journal: "When Patient Becomes Teacher," "How to Harpoon a Vein"
Pulse: "Snow Blind"
Rattle: "Midwifing My Father"
Retirement, Lifespan Vol 10: "Three Years Later"
Slipstream: "Unraveling the Mystery"

Please note: The poems in this book are based on actual events that took place during my nursing career. However, details and names have been altered to protect privacy.

* * *

My deep gratitude to the patients and families that I had the honor of caring for during my career, as well as to my heroic and amazing fellow nurses. Thank you, Terry Ehret, Sandé Anfang, and Catharine Clark-Sayles, for your keen eye and invaluable assistance in editing and helping me birth this collection. To the members of my writing groups—Monday Poets and Wellspring Writers—thank you for the many years of encouragement, friendship, and general awesomeness.

Praise for *Standing in Their Fire*

Shawna Swetech's powerful collection burns with the passion of a nurse dedicated to her calling. "To be a nurse is to be in their fire: the diseased, the incised, the dying." These poems are drawn from decades in nursing and chart her progress from a student attending a near-disaster ER case to a senior nurse overwhelmed by increasing documentation. Throughout, her compassion shines as she writes about patients desperately ill and grieves for them in moments, crying in the supply room with prayers "may these words/be caring hands, a lifeline of lines." In the third section, she writes of retirement and turns to nature for solace and healing in graceful poems that evolve into free-flowing forms. Anyone who has worked in medicine will resonate with these poems. Anyone who has experienced illness will take comfort in this portrait of nurse who has been willing to stand in fire for them.

—Catharine Clark-Sayles, MD, author of *The Telling, the Listening* and *Brats*

Standing in Their Fire is a powerhouse of a collection. Swetech leads the reader on a fantastic voyage through the body of the nursing experience. We can taste the profundity of what it means to witness and care—for the patient as well as the healer. The opening poem bookends the trajectory of a life's work: I didn't know / how willingly / I'd share their burden. / I didn't know / how willingly / I'd burn. The linguistic choices are carefully crafted to chime on an auditory as well as intellectual/emotional level. The poem "Drowning" makes exquisite use of onomatopoeia. This collection is deeply embedded in the marrow of the experience of one who followed a deep calling.

—Sandra Anfang, author of *Finishing School* and *Rara Avis*

Contents

In Their Fire   15

I. Of Pale Cells and Broken Shells

Rust   19
Dichotomy   20
In Flames   21
To the 35-Year-Old in Room 519   22
Drowning   23
Lifelines   24
The Secret Room   25
Of Pale Cells and Broken Shells   26
Good Medicine   27
Better than a Box of Chocolates   28
When Patient Becomes Teacher   29
What I Love at Work   30
A Seasoned Nurse   31
How to Harpoon a Vein   32

II. Lighting the Way Over

Calling Faith   35
Letting Him Go   36
Bone Structure   37
Rivulets of Rain   38
Morphine as Mercy   40
Lighting the Way Over   41
On Silent Wings   42
Death Lodge in Room 512   43
Bearing Witness   44
American Sunset   45

Murmuration for the Deceased   46
Rituals   47

III. Unraveling the Mystery

Crying in the Break Room at 10 a.m.   51
Your shift is over   52
Cat-a-Tonic   53
Plate Spinning   54
Snow-Blind   57
Staff Meeting Circumlocution   59
Down the Rabbit Hole   60
Unraveling the Mystery   61
Being My Own Patient   62
Midwifing My Father   64
After a Nurse Friend Takes Her Life   66
Mercy Missions   67

IV. Marrying Shadow to Light

Words   71
At the Riverbank   72
To Heal Your Wounds   73
Body, Celestial   74
The Secret to Life   75
Into a Colorless Unknown   76
Be Your Own Good Doctor   78
Flight   79
First Anniversary of the Last Shift, 9/20/2021   80
Three Years Later   81

How to Keep On   82
The Heart of the Matter   83

Afterword   85

In Their Fire

8 a.m. rounds,
stethoscope in hand.
The endless rooms of patients,
broken-boned or cancer-filled,
their fear and pain a bleeding river
I can never staunch.

To be a nurse
is to be in their fire:
the diseased, incised, dying.
I didn't know
what I was signing up for
thirty-five years ago,
the shift after shift
familiar scent of sorrow,
theirs and mine.

I didn't know
how willingly
I'd share their burden.

I didn't know
how willingly
I'd burn.

I. Of Pale Cells and Broken Shells

Rust

Color of oxidized metal or the brown of fungus
on a rose leaf. Stainless steel won't corrode,
neither will plastic. But once, I ran my finger
over a spot of powdery bronze on a cast-iron skillet,
marveling how the color stained my skin.
Then, decades later, that rotation in the ER
during nursing school, when a young man
came in hemorrhaging from his mouth,
a few days post-tonsillectomy, spitting copious
volumes of blood into a pink washbasin.
We ran his gurney down the hall full speed,
banging through the metal doors of the OR
for emergent surgery before he bled out. Afterward,
I couldn't stop trembling, had to step outside
into the cool morning before helping clean up
the exam room: the burgundy splattered walls;
the fishing of paper towels from the basin
of coagulating, still-warm blood. I'll never forget
the sickening glisten of floating fat, the blood's
metallic odor, like copper or rusty iron.
The large, soft clots moving in the thick liquid
against my gloved hand. The roiling horror
of that very close call.

Dichotomy

Morning report: female, mid-thirties,
status post auto accident.
Guillotine amputation
of upper arm, open patella fracture
with subsequent wound infection.

9 AM dressing change:
my gloved hand inserts to the wrist
in a cavern of once-smooth calf muscle.
I pull out piece after piece of packing gauze,
thickly dripping with the foul, yellow byproducts
of pseudomonas and staph aureus.
Quickly, I lay in sterile 4x4's,
wind the white stockinette around and over.

Next assessment: neat black sutures
poke like bristling hairs from what's left
of the right arm, of this single mother of five.
What caused the high speed, single-car rollover
and how will she manage now?
A growing lump in my throat
shifts my gaze out the narrow fourth floor window
and for a moment, I imagine myself out there
among the old grapevines, their gnarled
finger-bones branching skyward
as crisp autumn wind-waves
weave through my hair
. . . but I have to refocus.

I have to be professional.

I have to keep going.

In Flames

Images of the inferno raging home to home
in our drought-desiccated state. Fifteen minutes
to get out, one man cries barely time to grab the wife,
the dog, the computer. Wildlife, forests, schools,
family treasures, the history of entire towns
and 50,000 acres—all gone. Feeling sick,
I turn from the T.V. to my patient, yellow
and fresh out of a coma, with his gristly liver
and ballooned belly.

What's your plan to stay sober? I ask.
Don't have one, he says.
I throw every lifesaver I know: 12 Step info,
in-patient and out-patient programs. Stories
from my own life—husband twenty years clean,
our two alcoholic siblings who didn't make it.
Then, my best analogy: how not having a plan
is like standing on the beach in California,
sure you can make the swim to Hawaii.
You jump in, kick and kick, but soon
the struggling starts. Too late, you realize
you've forgotten nourishment, a support crew,
some kind of map. His dark eyes flick over me,
quickly return to the screen.

You need tools, I say. *This is life and death.
You can't keep doing what hasn't worked,
hoping for a miracle. I'll get the social worker,
we'll set you up with the help you need.*

He stares at the orange plumes pummeling
the night sky, red ash burnishing the wind.
No. I don't want it, he finally mutters.

To the 35-Year-Old in Room 519

It's almost 7 am; you're probably waking now
as night nurses hustle around, finishing up.

I'm driving in for my morning shift, hoping
the benzos are working and you aren't

in four-point restraints again. So many things
about the body you don't likely know, perhaps

don't need to—like the heart's Purkinje fibers,
the kidney's glomerular filtration rate, the salt

concentration in tears. Have you heard
of cytokines, how alcohol kicks Kupffer cells

into overdrive, ruins the liver? I asked
how many glasses of wine you drink a day,

and you said a couple—I wasn't referring
to sixteen-ounce tumblers. But you should know

why your belly is bloated, your eyes jaundiced,
and why you vomit blood: ascites, cirrhosis,

portal hypertension, the ooze of esophageal varices—
created bottle by bottle and year after year.

But what I really want to know is this:
will you step off the knife edge in time

before your slow,
                       slow suicide succeeds?

Drowning

In the break room
air conditioner's

> *Shhhh Shhhhh Shhhhhh*

like waves rolling, crashing.
Not like sounds from the patient
I just left, a back-of-the-throat
gurgle—every exhalation
like a breaching whale.
Not like yesterday, her last
coherent words to me

> *Nurse . . . am I going to die?*

Someone, please tell me
what makes a person drink
until their body drowns
in its own poison—
when the hand bringing death
to the lips could stop, but won't.

Tell me why that hand
keeps on and on until
comatose and liver-failed
a forty-year-old
becomes a beached shell
on a white sheet shoreline.

Lifelines

Though it's too late, liver fatty
and double-sized, I spike the poly bag
with clear tubing, watch the white
0.22-micron filter fill with packed red cells.

And though the whites of his eyes are yellow
as two risen suns, I plug into the IV port,
set the infusion pump with rate and volume,
run blood into his vein

per protocol—knowing, soon as it's finished,
he'll leave AMA, binge and be right back
in the ER. Excusing myself, I cross the hall
and slip into the supply room,

quietly close the heavy door so no one
will see me crying for this young man,
his addictive life—sick with sorrows
another transfusion won't treat.

I pull a scrap of paper from my uniform
pocket, and pen a poem-prayer for metanoia:
May my words be caring hands, a lifeline
of lines pulling you safely home.

The Secret Room

You left me here! I'm going to report you to the manager! she shouts, as I enter the room, clean linens in hand.

But I was on my fifteen-minute break, the other nurses were helping you, I stammer. Her accusations, my calm reasoning, as the black of her pupils grow storm-wild. *FUCK YOU! GO AWAY—I DON'T WANT TO TALK TO YOU!* she screeches, whipping my bare arm with the corner hem of her hospital gown.

Has she forgotten the dozens of trips I made into her room today, giving pills, pain meds, IV antibiotics, drawing blood from her implanted port for drug levels so the pharmacist can mix up the right doses? The hours spent at her bedside transfusing blood and platelets, checking and rechecking vital signs—so she won't bleed out after chemo stopped the work of her bone marrow? How many cups of coffee I brought her, with a splash of milk, just as she likes it? How many times we lifted her to the commode, held her so she wouldn't fall? Dabbed cream on her irritated tissues—gently, as we would for a small child? Months in a metal-ringed hospital room is a long time, in pain and not knowing if she'll ever get home again.

But her words . . . her fury-blind eyes. She can't see us in the hallway, consoling each other after her explosions. Or on a day off, lying on the couch in our bathrobes all day, skeletal and exhausted, shut away in the secret room of our closed heart. How our families suffer when we're too gutted to come out.

She can't imagine how cyclones of dread tear through every cell when we show up for the next shift, and find her name listed in our assignment.

Of Pale Cells and Broken Shells

Diagnosis: femur head fracture,
Medical history: advanced vascular dementia.
Far distant history: degrees in psychology,
yoga, teaching—before her brain folded itself
into an intricate origami of pale cells
and broken shells.
    I have asky open on you! MOMMMyyyyy!
    One of the powerful, she shouts.
    BOBBIE! Uhhhh . . .. BobbiEEEE!
    Bye, I'll never find those kids.
Meal tray in hand, I sit next to the bed.
She's a good eater, approving *Mmmm*
follows every spoonful of chocolate pudding
I feed her. *Oh, excuse me!* she says
after brushing my arm. The small wave
of lucidity quickly disappears in the murk
between hemispheres, neuronal tangles.
    Heaven's gone afar, if you'd clear it . . .
    I'll fall you for four! I wish my father
    would go thee!
Morning rounds: she's holding her nose,
tells the psychiatrist she's under water.
He charts: Thought form: disorganized.
Thought content: impoverished, irrelevant.
Her eyes, blue as sea fans,
search the ceiling as she sips at the air
as if through a snorkel—as if swimming
toward a memory's memory
on some faraway shore.
    What is the time when you get to tour
    the time? Don't wash the washes.
    What the water the water went through
    to find you!

Good Medicine

Today, dashing room to room on our busy medical unit,
I fell in love again with the calling of care-giving,
and with each patient receiving our medicine—remedies
to cool the fires of sepsis; to make the dragons of pain lie still;
to conscript red and white blood cells, swelling their fighting
ranks. I fell in love with the physical body, finite and frail,
and how illness and breakings can ignite a path to emotional and
spiritual transformation. Like when I held the hand
of a patient crying, awaiting cancer surgery. Sitting on the edge
of her bed, I said, Let's take five breaths together. Inhaling
and exhaling the leaden air, we held each other's gaze—deeply,
one human being to another, the light slowly shifting in her eyes.
Sometimes, the best prescription isn't a shot or pill.
It's the good medicine of kindness. Of care. Of love.

Better than a Box of Chocolates

Rolling by on a steel gurney, a transfer from the local trauma unit. Gingerly, the ambulance guys slide him to the hospital bed, as I assess the tibia/fibula fracture site, surgically repaired with an open reduction, internal fixation. I note the swelling, the clean ace wraps twisting from foot to mid-thigh, his warm exposed toes. The scabbed road rashes, the bruises purpling his body. I bring ice water, pain meds, elevate his leg onto fluffed pillows. Then ask admission questions, my fingers flittering over the computer keys like a concert pianist. Looking up, I notice the way he's watching me, the slow-blinking half-stare. He tells me he was riding on a side street when someone ran a red light. Says he's seventy years old, never been in the hospital before, never even been sick. Ridden a motorcycle for over forty years. In his still gaze, I think I see fear: the narrow miss of death's swinging scythe. I take his hand, say, *You are going to get through this. You will heal.* He replies, *You know what the worst thing is?* I shake my head, bracing for some terrible revelation. *The doctor says I won't be able to ride my motorcycle for another two years!*

> My ageist notions
> take wing and fly
> out the open window

When Patient Becomes Teacher

7:15 am. Report from the night nurse: Male, Stage 4 decubitus ulcer and septicemia. Paraplegia from a long-ago spinal wound, bilateral above-the-knee amputations, colon cancer with colostomy placement, permanent suprapubic urinary catheter, triple lumen central line IV. Orders for extensive three times a day dressing changes, and strict bed rest in supine position only. Ahead, weeks of around-the-clock antibiotics, then more surgery . . .

8:15 am. Morning rounds. *Knock, knock,* I say, peeking around the curtain, clipboard clutched to my chest. There, floating atop the special Fluidair mattress, is the patient—and just the upper half of a body. Except for a few wrinkles in the sheets, the lower portion of the bed is without contour. I expect someone with a broken spirit, a chronically sour disposition, rightfully earned. But when he sees me, his wide smile and palpable happiness lights the drab room —a sudden sunrise shining right into me.

What I Love at Work

The morning stethoscope ritual: lifting it
from around my neck, warming its bell
on my hands so the patient won't jump.
Inserting the gray rubber tips into my ears,
opening the back of the patient's gown
then resting my left hand on their shoulder.
Take a deep breath, I say, then auscultate
lung fields between scapulae, moving down
the spine, one side to the other: the tidal flow
of critical gasses exchanging, the blow and breach
of the chest's twin whales inhaling, exhaling.
I listen for bibasilar crackles of heart failure,
coarse congestion of pneumonia, wheeze of asthma.
Egophony, rattles, rhonchi, stridor. Or silence—
from emphysema, cancer, a lobectomy.
The overlay of intestinal digestive borborygmi:
the clicks and gurgles of peristalsis echoing
through the belly. All the while
I'm marveling at the body's largest organ:
noting skin color, tattoos, scars, tan lines,
wrinkles, hair, visible ribs, soft fleshy rolls.
Thousands of people, thousands of bodies—
what I love is the brief, breathtaking intimacy
of eavesdropping on organs performing
their moment-to-moment miracles.

A Seasoned Nurse

Every kind of effluvia and excreta a body produces
has spilled or splashed on my shoes, my uniforms,
my hands—all those germy little bombs dropletting
into eyes, nose and mouth these past thirty-five years.
Right now, for example, I'm in the break room
about to have lunch. I look down, and there
on my pant leg is a silver-dollar-sized blop
of somebody's blood. You're probably horrified
but it's so nothing next to things I've seen:
infected incisions, gangrenous black toes, wounds
alive with maggots. I make a mental note
to Spray-n-Wash it later, as I dive into my green salad
and leftovers. I don't even get up to clean it off.

How to Harpoon a Vein

Look at the vein. Is it prominent and soft, or fine
like a dark thread, hidden under spongy layers
of adipose? Will a tourniquet make it harden and roll
or will pressure's bind burst the blue line,

blood purpling the tissues? And the skin—is it thick
like tanned leather, or onion-skin thin, a pale veil
separating the inner and outer world. Look and feel
but trust your fingers more than your eyes.

Exude confidence. Swipe the target with alcohol,
twirl the angiocath's steel stylet. To the Gods
of IV Starts, direct a plea into the electrical outlet
behind the bed: *PLEASE! Let me get in, first stick!*

Tell your patient to imagine their vein is fat and soft.
Don't think of stabbing flesh, causing pain. Tell yourself
it's a lifeless fish, not someone's arm. The needle
is just a tiny harpoon and you are Ahab.

Exude additional confidence. Hold your breath,
and bevel up, drive the sharp tip down and in.
Does blood flash into the hub? If not, swear silently.
If so, quickly slide the plastic cannula in

and pull the needle out. Don't poke yourself!
Attach the IV tubing, place an antiseptic patch
at the insertion site, then a see-through dressing.

Turn the pump on, set the rate. If the gods
were in a good mood today, bow a little.
Give thanks.

II. Lighting the Way Over

Calling Faith

How much time do I have? she asks.
I hope she means before dinner
or until the next pain meds are due.
But when she reaches for my hand,
I see a deeper plea in the circular black
of her pupils. Rising out of myself,
I become Nightingale or any nurse,
at any bedside across time, giving care
to the dying—who ask not for numbers
or days, but sacrament.

No one really knows, I tell her.
Do you feel ready?

No, not yet, she says, softly crying.

Then it's not time, I reply.
*We have more say-so about dying
than we think.*

I fight to steady my voice by observing
the hand squeezing mine. The crease
at the inner elbow with its IV site
and clear cover dressing. The pink drop
of fluid where the needle pierces the skin.

*We all know we have to leave one day,
but it's still hard,* I say, looking into
her brown eyes. *For thousands of years
the sacred texts have told us our souls
are eternal, that there's more beyond this life.
Even if we can't see with our human eyes,
we have to believe—*
       that's why they call it faith.

Letting Him Go

As a people, we abhor finality.
Take the unresponsive patient
in room 312, skin stretched
like cellophane over bones thinned
with unheard truth.

The family says *Do everything.*
So, doctors order new meds,
another too-late CAT scan.
We poke him with needles
for more blood tests, thread
a weighted feeding tube
into his nostril and down
to his looping bowels.

No one sees the shadows
of liminal light falling
all around the room,
or his soul's subtle symptoms
of preparation. No one notices
his hands, prayer-posed
in the center of his chest—
hands that clearly say

  I am dying

    I am dying

      I am dying

Bone Structure

the bones have hollowed
become thin and see-through

      their osseous structure disordered
      by leukemia's fulminant blaze

red marrow crowded out
now   the metamorphosis is complete

      from the doorway   chemo bag in hand
      I pause   observe him heavily reclined

in medicated sleep   the charcoal hollow
of eye sockets   skin stretched skeletal

      over craggy cliffs of cheek
      the thin sticks of his arms

angling straight out from the shoulders
in a perfect T   I half expect

      that right in front of me   he'll wing
      up from the bed   and fly into the ethers

Rivulets of Rain

cochlear shells shut
saline rises in my eyes, spills
too much   too much
I fall blue   into blue   into blue
relentless waves
on your shoreline
hospice-colored clouds
shadows   transparent
now I see   into you   your skin
your loss, uncountable
years of pain
so that I too
turn translucent
bare
-ly visible
oh god   oh   god   I can't
this break
-ing this sorrow
its full-stone weight
crushing the perimeter
of my heart
Now—I must
quickly quickly
to slim window
ray of winter-
solstice light
and with my eyes
trace the rivulets
of rain

weep
—ing
weep
—ing
down
  the
pane

Morphine as Mercy

They've all decided it's time—
the patient, family, doctors.
I prepare the morphine drip bag,
IV solutions, the med pump.
But when I enter the hospital room,
her husband of sixty years looks up,
cries, *"Already?"*

The narcotic begins its slow descent
down the thin tube coiling into her arm.
He brings her bluish hand to his lips,
all the while watching her heaving,
smoke-ruined lungs fight
for every last molecule blasting
from the high-flow oxygen mask.
I blink back tears as he brushes
a stray hair from her cheek.

Starched sheets and window light
illuminate his face, the strain
of grief. His eyes—so full of love,
so full of what will come next.

Lighting the Way Over

for P.K, in memoriam

Midwives to the dying, nurses carry,
step by step, the ones coming to their end.
These patients, their families, all their stories
and how they leave this world, live on in us.
But hers . . . went in deep.

Fifty-five is too young, we said,
week after week—hoping with each
new medication, she'd finally turn the corner.
But cell by cell, tumors grew, building
their excruciating temples in lymph nodes,
organs and bones. Still, her kindness, grace
as the forest of her respiratory system
burnt down—lungs so full of char and leavings,
gasses barely exchanged.

"I can't breathe! I can't breathe!"
Her cries a terrible sorrow we couldn't unhear.
We watched as she shrank to shadowlands,
cancer stealing every morsel it could find.

Each time we answered her call light,
our hearts turned leaden. Our small,
final acts became gestures of faith, of love.
Became lights to illuminate the wide bridge
she'd soon pass over from this radiant world
to the next.

On Silent Wings

thin, tissue-covered branch
of bone and sinew
the knot of elbow
protruding
from a snow bank
of sheets, blankets
      —Oh, but those eyes
those eyes
are what pierce me
the dark pupil portals
to a nameless eternity
I fall into
with every blink
exquisite mirror
of fragile beauty
this worn glove
called *body*
      —see how easy, they say
when the time is right
you simply slip out

and

fly
              y
         a
  a   w

Death Lodge in Room 512

Native American in her 60s, hospitalized
for stasis ulcers and chronic illness
sits in a bedside chair as I cleanse and dress
her leg wounds. We talk about her life
and how she feels, now that she's improving.

Midday, a small group of native elders arrive.
Closing her door, they drum and sing tribal songs.
The scent of a smoldering sage wafts
into the hallway.

After an hour, the visitors float silently
toward the elevator like leaves on a fall breeze.
My patient is back in bed, eyes closed,
covers pulled to her chin.

Later, when I enter her room to give
the next round of scheduled meds, I notice
she hasn't moved. I think she's sleeping.
But her skin is a colorless cool.

How did she go from being fully alive
to dead in the space of just a few hours?
Then I realize: She chose this.

Her people came to smudge and pray her spirit
into the next world, with a ceremony of passage.

This is how to die, I tell myself.

It doesn't have to be so hard.

Bearing Witness

Under my stethoscope, the heart
is a fluttering, restless creature. Her gray eyes,
open and unfocused, see nothing. Just yesterday
we talked of dark chocolate, her homeland in Italy.
But today, a sweaty halo fans
across the pillow, encircling the tidy white curls.
Today, she is dying.

I sit on the bed, hold her cool hand,
feel the vein's dark thread, barely palpable.
I think of my calling as a nurse
and how many times
I've helped the backward birth of a soul
from form to formless.
I remember my mother's passage,
how her hand curled into mine, just like this.

They're paging me now, but I won't go.
I'm staying with her to the end
of her seventy-five years.
Until with the breath's last outrush
her chest falls,
and doesn't rise again.

American Sunset

like the plastic bag scene in the movie
American Beauty

my patient's hands flutter and spin
in the air   artful and lovely

as IV tubes fly between forearm
and morphine pump

I touch his shoulder   bend to his ear
tell him he's taking a journey today

alone   no family   no bedside vigil
so, I stand in   as final witness

hour after hour   till he's still
and colorless as salt   sun setting

on his dementia   and eighty-seven years
but no prayers   no final words

for this mother's child   grandfather
decorated war veteran

one last glimpse at his kind face
as we zipper shut the body bag

slide the load to the gurney
away to the morgue   the crematory

where tissue and bone   of no further use
whirl to a flurry of ash

Murmuration for the Deceased

Dressed in draping blacks, their arms
are dark wings, flapping and flailing
as wails crescendo down the narrow
hospital corridor. Gold bracelets
jangling, they beseech their gods,
hold to each other in the bright
pattern of their grief.
A few doors
down,
another family
perches on bedside chairs
like discreet brown doves, tidy
in their tissue-dabbing of noses
and eyes, as the stroke's fatal stain
claims their loved one. Only quiet
murmurs of witness to the final rise
and fall of her hollow breastbone.

Rituals

She lies on the hospital bed next to the stilled body,
murmurs *I love you, darling . . . I love you, darling,*
kisses his cooling cheek over and over.
Their two adult daughters hold hands, perched
on brown folding chairs, every fiber straining
toward them.

    And though I recognize the skin's wax-pallor,
    I center my stethoscope on his chest anyway,
    where the *lub-dup, lub-dup* should be

but isn't. All the air squeezes from the room
as they wait for me to utter what no one ever wants
to hear, those seven little nuclear bombs:
    His heart has stopped—I'm so sorry.

Back at the nurses' station, the wife
sits across from me as I call the doctor.
Pushing the cottony curls from her face,
she begins the new widow's ritual:
    reminiscing about the deceased.
    How they met in high school,
    together over sixty years.
    The wonderful father he was.

When she sobs, *I can't imagine life without him . . .*
my stomach tightens, a sure sign I'm slipping
into sorrow's thick bog. But no. I can't.
The mortician's coming and there's paperwork
to finish. I have to phone the organ donor hotline.
The ER is calling report for my next admission,
coming soon as his room's been cleaned.

Breathe slow and deep, I tell myself.
Focus on her silk blouse, the rich colors
of turquoise and emerald green. Watch
the distracted motion of her hands
twisting a wet Kleenex into the shape
of a mushroom cloud. If my tears brim,
I'll hide my hands under the counter
and press the fingernails of my right hand
into the palm of the left—just underneath
my thinning platinum band.

III. Unraveling the Mystery

Crying in the Break Room at 10 a.m.

Maybe I'm crying because this doctor, this male authority, shouted in the middle of the nurse's station when I told him his patient was actively dying, that we needed comfort care orders. He yelled at me to stop pushing him, then dismissed me like I was some green, know-nothing nurse, not a twenty-year veteran reporting objective signs—and what I knew in my gut. When I didn't want to heave her almost lifeless body onto one more hard gurney, for the CT scan he just ordered. He was wrong, but I lost my voice. Could barely eke out *I understand*—when I didn't.

Maybe I'm crying because of what I witnessed: grown sons silently dabbing their eyes at the bedside of their comatose mother. Their grieving father hunched over the side rails, clinging to the hand of his wife of fifty-five years. How they all watched the hissing oxygen blow like a hurricane into the mask, as she struggled for every ragged breath.

Maybe their pain reached out, traced the edges of my own: watching helplessly as my mother died from lung cancer just like this. Imagining my family gathered around my bed one day when I am the one passing.

Maybe after decades of nursing the sick, the dying, the mourning families, my tears couldn't wait for one more shift to end.

Your shift is over

but you can't shake the whirling misery
of what you witnessed: All those patients
and grief-pale families: that seventeen-year-old
in liver failure, transferring to the big San Francisco
hospital, with only two possible outcomes:
transplant or death. His parents pressing
against the wall as he rolls by on the gurney,
anguish rising like palpable steam.
A young woman readmitted for uncontrolled pain.
The man felled by a stroke, unable to speak
a single word. Another, cancer's battle lost,
begging you to help him die. *Please, please . . .
give me something!* Discharging your favorite patient
home on hospice after two months in your care.
It wasn't supposed to be like this, you said, crying.
I was supposed to send you home in remission.
He held your hand when he left, shared
what he said was his life's final wisdom:
*In the end, love is all that matters—
it's all you take with you when it's over.*

Yet for you, it isn't over. The shell-shock
is deep, numbing. You still see them, hear them
calling out for you . . . *NURSE! NURSE!*
You cocoon in your blanket, pray for sleep's
anesthetic amnesia—but it doesn't work.
Finally, you try the Bathtub Ritual: two cups
of Epson salts, twenty drops of lavender
essential oil, stirred into the steaming water.
Submerged to your chin, you're finally able
to sob into a washcloth. You sit there so long
the water cools. You open the drain
and watch every last drop swirl away.

Cat-a-Tonic

    Twelve-hour shift completed
        twelve hours flitting room to room
like a wingless bird stopping only
      to peck peck peck
          at the computer
              before flying off
      to the med cart   the dressing cart
the pantry   grabbing clean linen
calling the doctor   giving a shot   a pill
      a tray of food   helping patients
        in and out of bed
      giving hope   giving answers
talking   teaching   assessing
      rushing   room to room
          hour after hour.

At last, I pull into our dark driveway
cut the engine   close my eyes
feel the throb of knees and feet
fatigue's bone-deep hammer weight.
When I finally swing open the car door
Mr. Cake springs onto the jam   the motor
of his purr revs like a Big Rig pulling uphill.
Cradling him high up on my chest,
I bury my face in his long white fur
and pet him with both hands.

What better tonic, I ask you,
than that of a cat?

Plate Spinning

Sunday night, 1962. The Ed Sullivan Show.
  I'm perched on the couch watching
        the
        black
        and
        white
        TV
        my
        nerves
        in knots
        as the
        plate
        spinner
        hurls
        himself
        pole
        to pole
        in time
        to the
        crazy
        circus
        music
        one
        wrist-
        flick
        away
        from
        all
        that
        china
        crashing
        to the
        floor.

Now it's Wednesday morning, day
shift. We're working in a hospital
        without
        enough
        staff.
        My
        stomach's
        knotted
        as I spin
        room
        to room
        giving
        meds
        trans-
        fusions
        meal trays
        answering
        call lights
        talking
        to docs
        families
        all the
        while
        trying to
        real-time
        chart
        in com-
        puters
        that always
        need
        rebooting.

It's not if but when everything will
  crash, a "fact finding" called
      about
      why
      the
      patient
      fell
      meds
      passed
      late pain
      reassess-
      ments
      missed
      education
      not done
      document-
      ation
      incomplete
      and why
      overtime
      is up
      when
      patient
      satisfact-
      ion scores
      are so
      low
      and
      sick
      calls
      are
      so
      high.

Snow-Blind

Avalanche dream—heavy breakage of trees, boulders ripped from their footings. Chunks of ice bouncing past as the swirling white mass picks up speed. I'm running, running, running but can't stay ahead of it. Lungs burn, tears stream from the effort, the strain. Glazed in sweat, I wake up to the blare of alarm clock, hurriedly dress and drive to the hospital.

Time speeds into the day. It's busy. We're short-staffed again. One patient has to go for a test, has pain, needs medicine while another has to be readied for early surgery. She's scared, needs pain meds, pre-op teaching, a guided imagery CD to help her cope. Another, detoxing and crying. Someone else can't breathe, coughs blood, the doctor must be notified STAT. Next room, a patient returns from inconclusive tests, she's worried, needs medicine for her nerves. They all want me to listen to their stories. Why the drinking started after her firstborn left for college—now the last is about to go. How long that man's been waiting for new lungs, says he's sorry someone must die first. Check clock. Pass meds. Better hurry. Discharge orders for another. I have to take the urinary catheter out first. Will she be able to pee on her own? Will pills work for her fractured femur, once I stop the morphine drip? Now another patient's going home, needs teaching. I haven't started charting, rated the patients' acuity or reassessed pain. Call lights flash. Everyone needs something: a bedpan, a lunch tray. The discharge nurse, a family member, the lab tech all want to talk to me right away.

A doctor demands I attend bedside rounds right NOW. I'm late. I'm running, running, running, hard as I can. The hallway is empty, everyone's busy, no one can help. I have to use the bathroom. My mouth is dry, where's my water. Any minute now, the break nurse will come to send me to lunch but I'm not hungry. My palms are sweating. I feel sick. Then disaster: I discover I've made a med error. Too late, I remember the nightmare, the déjà vu of panic, the total white-out of whirling snow I couldn't stay ahead of. The spinning and spinning through empty air.

Staff Meeting Circumlocution

RN: We need more help to care for the patients. Manager: Your numbers don't call for more help. *But the numbers come from our computer charting, and we can't chart because we're trying to answer call lights, give meds, and get patients up for meals.* Your ambulatory scores are too low. Patients aren't getting their teeth brushed three times a day. And the hospital's patient satisfaction score is dropping. *But we can't give satisfying care if we don't have enough people to give the care.* Well, the financing department dropped our budget to six patients a day even though we average sixteen. We're trying to get emergency money because the budget won't change for a year. Right now, we can't hire more people, and thirty-six staff are out on medical leave. So . . . can you stay overtime, come in early, or pick up some extra shifts? *But what about work/life balance? Care isn't safe or good coming from exhausted people, who're working all this overtime—day after day without enough help. We need more staff to care for the patients.* Your numbers don't call for more help. *But we can't get the numbers up because we can't chart. We're too busy taking care of the patients.*

        birds droop on thin twigs
        rain dries before hitting ground
        useless summer squall

*Lines directly quoted from my Staff Meeting notes, after the implementation of the new EPIC staffing system.

Down the Rabbit Hole

I'm determined to have a good day, so I wore my duty shoes by Alegria, which is Spanish for happiness. Their bright colors and embossed concentric circles seem to spin as I scurry along. When a patient admires them, I tell her I like a festive shoe at work. When she comments on my Alice-in-Wonderland printed scrub top, I say, well, I never know what rabbit hole I'll fall in when I'm on shift. Soon after, cacophony and chaos as the nurse's station fills up, everyone talking over each other. Call lights beep, IV pumps shriek, phones jangle at the desk and buzz in our pockets like swarms of mad hornets. BING BONG BING BONG BING BONG. A man with dementia sets off his bed alarm and we race to his room to keep him from falling. I look at my watch. Time to squeeze in bedside rounds with the care team between scheduled morning med passes. Colors swirl and swim on the periphery as nurses and assistants run past each other in the halls, no time for eye contact—until *CODE BLUE* blares over the paging system and we freeze like rabbits, mid-stride. Smiles plastered on, we mustn't forget management's latest decree: sit on the patient's bed when doing hourly "authentic rounds," so they'll feel like we're really listening. Because pleasing the members is a must for 5-star ratings—or it might be off with our proverbial heads. Tick Tick Tick Tick Tick Tick. Need to get charting before 11:00 A.M. to accrue points so the next shift isn't understaffed—but every time I try, it's interruption after interruption until even the interruptions get interrupted. Oh, thank God—it's almost lunch time. I can't wait to sit down and kick these happy shoes off my unhappy feet.

Unraveling the Mystery

Standing beside an institutional bed,
I hear myself ask, *"Do you want to stay—*
or are you ready to die?" My eyes fly open
in the dark of my bedroom. Is this question
for one of my patients—or for myself?
In the morning, I ask the dream to speak
through magazine images I choose at random,
collage onto a painted page: a Timber wolf
howling into darkness. Owl mid-flight, looking
over his shoulder, haunting eyes on the hunt.
Grim Reaper presiding over a barren landscape,
scythe extended in one hand, inviting with the other.

Then I add more—a drawing of a man's feet,
one great toe wound with a fading vine, the other
tied with an undertaker's tag. Two banded snakes
in a yellow, black, and red twist, in the shape
of a medical caduceus hovering over x-rayed bones.
A dark arm extending from a clouded realm,
pointing to three words: Unraveling the Mysteries.

But of what—life? Death's borderland?
When I contemplate illness, modern medicine
and all its promises, all I can think of
is the Buddha's blunt truth: the cause
of suffering is life; the cause of death, birth.
And how every day on some level,
we make the choice: *Should I stay?*
Or am I ready to go?

Being My Own Patient

Seven days now, I marinate in pneumonia's fevered brine,
slave to a microscopic universe—unable
in all my human brilliance,
to stop them at my body's castle gates.
I've become vector, carrier, factory,
as they steal my cells to feed their mutating masses.

I could die tonight, ablaze with the pyre they've set,
103.1° and still rising.
(A virus cares not if it kills the host)
Sinus tachycardia: heart slamming the walls
of my chest in a fever-driven pace.
Every muscle, a crushing ache.

Should I let the fever do its job, or suppress it,
burn the bacteria alive?
Those little monsters are terrible gods.
I take the meds, pack my armpits
and groin with ice bags.

Have I peed enough? Are my lips chapped?
DO NOT GET DEHYDRATED,
the inner nurse commands.
I drink and drink between burning bouts of coughing.

Afraid to close my eyes,
I see in the bedroom's night-light glow
my favorite oil painting on the wall in front of me:
the sweeping Pacific coastline above Jenner.
I imagine floating
in that cool, healing sea
saltwater drawing illness out of me.
Upper body elevated on two pillows,
I finally sleep.

In the morning, a second sun rises:
my temperature is normal.
I did not enter the palace
of bleached bones
and darkness.

I'm alive.

Midwifing My Father

for L. Brooks Staton, 1/15/1915–6/14/2005

I sit alone at his convalescent home bedside.
He is not responsive, eyes unfocused and unblinking.
On the inner wrist, below the thumb, his pulse is rapid, thready.
His breath is heavy, and wet with a death rattle—a sound
only recognized by one familiar with life's end.
I've helped deliver soul from body many times, but not like this.
I watch the warm life recede from his hands, tan replaced
by dusky mottle. Heart hammering under the sunken sternum,
I see him struggle to stay, as he balls his fists, pummels the air—
grimacing and flinching. Does he imagine it's WWII, when his
ship the USS Quincy, was torpedoed and sank in the dead of night?
Is he fighting his way topside, though fire, over fallen bodies,
before jumping overboard into the burning oil on the black sea
of the South Pacific? Or fending off angels, here to spirit him
away? I take his hands, and lie across his chest, pressing him
with all my weight. *Dad, I'm here—I'm here, Dad, it's okay . . .*
I kiss the chisel of his cheekbone, telling him stories
of good times, like when we went to see Sandy Koufax
pitch the World Series at Dodger Stadium, 1965.
I remind him of the playhouse he built for me

in the backyard, the one that later became the Monkey House
for Dondy, our gibbon ape. I talk about other pets,
how he taught Omar, the mynah bird, to say, *I'm a dirty bird!*
And our old dog, Tippy, throwing himself at the front door
when the mail dropped through the slot. I know he still hears me
because he nods his head slightly after each tale.
But then he flails against the air again.
So, I talk about Sunday afternoons at Knott's Berry Farm,
when he'd give me a dollar to pan for gold. Summer evenings,
those grunion hunts at Seal Beach. The time he pushed me in a
grocery cart along the bumpy wood planks of the old Rainbow
Pier, downtown Long Beach. I tell him things weren't perfect—
we made mistakes, but we did the best we could.

His breath grows irregular. I tell him to let go,
that Mother is waiting. I plead for God to help him.
At 1:59 p.m. he coughs so hard and so deep,
he bends forward at the waist, trunk lifting up off the bed.
Every bit of air rushes from his lungs.
His body falls back onto the pillow.

He doesn't breathe back in.

After a Nurse Friend Takes Her Life

—for J.O.

Flying onto the freeway, accelerating to seventy,
the day lurches forward on a tread of determination,
a winged desperation: I must, must do something
of substance. Because another day unblinking and
stupefied is like life and death jaggedly juxtaposed
in memory of muscle and mind.

> *. . . how does one come to crave their end*
> *the blankness   the slack of body line*
> *telling no one   but google*
> *a plan, best rope   pick date*
> *time   tie rope to door-*
> *knob   toss over to other*
> *side   settle necklace*
> *of noose thickly*
> *under chin &*
> *kick loose*
> *into the*
> *alone*
> *of thin*
> *air*

I turn onto a side road, driving under a verdant canopy
of trees. Am stunned by the leafy dapple of the sky's
blue expanse. After wildfires last fall, I was certain
the sorrowful scorch of trunk and limbs was forever,
I stopped looking up.

> *. . . maybe*
> *this is how*
> *she came to*
> *her want: surety*
> *of forever; the stop-*
> *ping; the never again*
> *daring to look up back up.*

Mercy Missions

A nurse friend shows me a photo in her cell phone, from her medical mission to Zimbabwe: simple buildings, trees, and something like a river. But it's not water. It's a winding line of people, five and six wide, stretching from where she stands then disappearing over the far horizon. They walk for days, she says, waiting in line day and night for care at the temporary clinic volunteers set up. Each one carries a smudged brown book: a complete medical record, handwritten, with every illness, procedure, appointment they've ever had. In five days, they treat more than 13,000 people—surgeries, wounds, chronic illness, dental extractions, more. Each doctor sees over 500 people a day. I'm stunned. So opposite from the clean hospital where I work, with our five-patient assignments, computers, every possible supply at our fingertips.

What moved you most on the trip, I ask. The twins, she replies, telling me how she scrubbed for a caesarean, the mother not sure how long she'd been pregnant, the surprise twin boys. The head nurse, a volunteer more than thirty years, called them grunters: preemies without enough surfactant in their lungs to keep the air sacs open. They won't make it, the senior nurse tells her. But my friend doesn't give up. She works the only oxygen mask from the only tank at the clinic, from baby to baby. After the first one dies, she holds the mask on the other until a new doctor comes in. He rolls the oxygen tank away

to help an unresponsive 10-year-old boy, infected with TB and HIV. Later, she grieves with the doctor—the older child died too. My friend holds out her phone again, shows me the tiny twins, still warm and breathing. They'd have made it in a modern hospital, she says. This photo is the only record that they were ever on this earth at all.

IV. Marrying Shadow to Light

Words

Voiced
or silent
on a page
words are panacea,
like the quench
of a late-summer rain
flowing
over the parched
earth of us,
or encircling our bodies
like warm arms
on a cool
autumn night.

Just listen . . .
even a tiny poem
has healing hands.

At the Riverbank

I kneel down,
    drink of the clear
        elixir, like a cool
            flowing medicine
        over my parched lips,
tongue. Why is it
I've forgotten
  about the river
      and its ever-present
          current—how freely
      it nourishes my roots?
    Why have I
  forgotten roots,
the under-earth tangle
    where yours
        meet mine?
          And this place
     we come from,
    the soil of settled
stardust, old
  and deep.
    Come,
       rest here
          beside me,
            tell me
        of your thirst.
     Pull water
    into
      your
       tap root.
     Sip
    from your
   cupped
    hands.

To Heal Your Wounds

1. From a pearl somewhere on the ocean floor,
a translucent shimmer greater than the crush
of sorrows. Let the burdens you carry splinter
to shipwreck.

2. It's a matter of opening the soul's window
to light; of marrying that light to
the shadows you carry.

3. Every morning, the untied laces of another day
flap in the wind as the sun traverses hot
across the planet's blue gardens. Meanwhile,
blue whales migrate north and Canada Geese
navigate the Pacific Flyway.

4. Now mind is clear. Now heart is clear.
Hands, unclenched, hang loosely at your sides
and the bees clotting your throat have finally
flown on.

5. Outside, birds are speaking in tongues.
Trees shake their small green flags. Witness
the russet expanse of day—how stones assemble
themselves into cairns to mark the way.

6. Forget what's unfinished, not yet whole.
Cracks, chips, breakings: beauty's ragged
and imperfect art is everywhere you dare to look.

7. *Dare to look.*

Body, Celestial

*Beauty is only skin deep, but ugly goes clear
to the bone,* someone once quipped.

Well, I'm a nurse and a poet, and the bones I've seen
are white, lovely as a winter moon.

And the textured skin, dermis and epidermis fulfilling
their oath: everything kept in, everything else out.

What, may I ask, is more beauteous than the body,
its full miracle—every pulsing, electrified cell?

Muscles flexing, fingers moving, chambers
of the heart pumping 4,000 times an hour,

the five lobes of the lungs like a squeeze box,
playing oxygen to every organ? Over time,

it might be true, beauty dives to a deeper definition.
Burrows beneath scars, wrinkles, the pigmented spots

of earned wisdom. But let's be real: Life is no
beauty pageant. It's a split-second, cellular marathon

run to the end, when we finally lay it all down:
sinews, tissues, bones—everything

from metatarsals to cranium. With our last breath,
the light of us blooms on—into star, into nebula:

a body celestial, corpuscular and infinitely
so much more than merely beautiful.

The Secret to Life

Racing along
arms outstretched
and fingers feeling
everything,
your fast feet
bounce along
the rock-strewn
path. Life
is not just a walk
in shadow,
a daydream,
a fog.
The stars
in their wan
strange light
know you—
famished foreigner,
always searching
for the next feast
of meaning.
But even now
the corners
of your mouth
lift upward
and your eyes
crinkle at the corners:
somewhere deep down,
you know the secret
to life's short bliss:

Every day, bless the earth you walk on.
Every day, beautify all you'll leave behind.

Into a Colorless Unknown

Raven's grown older now. I watch her fly
        overhead, blue-black wings wide out

catching updrafts, each feather-finger moving
        by the workings of its own small muscle.

Feathers opening so that white sunlight alternates
        with black like a piano keyboard in flight.

Velocity, altitude change with the slightest of effort,
        because Raven has faith in the wind, in things

working perfectly: a free mouse the cat leaves
        on the driveway, a bit of leftover kibble

on the porch to pilfer. Well, I'm older now, too.
        My fingers are starting to fan open, to feel

for new directions as work life nears its natural
        end-stop. Who will I be then, without work?

The three-decade theme of my life, more central
        than family even, the always-ness

of that weekly schedule. Who will I be
        if not defined as registered nurse,

no longer an expert tasked with caring for others?
        Can I ride these new winds like Raven,

though dread creaks through my dreams
    like a hundred rusty hinges?

How will I navigate the wilderness
    of this colorless unknown?

Be Your Own Good Doctor

Take the healer's oath—to first, do no harm
to yourself. Become a doctor of downward dog,

of psoas stretch. Of hands in the soil, organic
garden greens and fresh salt air. Take daily

the good medicine of smile, your teeth free
of nicotine and wine stain. Be a doctor

of prayer hands and morning daimoku,
of food as medicine. Of plant-based,

of echinacea and elderberry and tincture
of a good night's sleep. Poultice of sunshine

and forest Shinrin-yoku. Make remedies
of kimchee and kraut, lap cat and henhouse.

Heal with word and water color, glue stick
and journal paper. Because who better

to nurture the abundant earth of you
than you?

Flight

Six months—no name tag, no alarm exploding
at 5 a.m. for an eight- or twelve-hour shift.
No patients, no call lights, no morning rounds,
or days of clock-tick panic.

> *What rising will salt my blood now,*
> *what sky will light the way? My self,*
> *blown open, remembering day by day,*
> *the feather and light bone I'm made of.*

Thirty-five years racing bedside to bedside
tending the sick, the wounded, the broken,
my career book-ended by pandemics:
AIDS in 1985, and Covid-19 in 2020.

> *Mornings, I am birdsong. Nights, I sleep free*
> *of nightmares: the stress-haunted faces,*
> *the hands pulling at me, the late meds, the work*
> *piling up . . . overtime I'll be in trouble for.*

My nursing uniforms, washed and folded
into two brown bags, fall over in the trunk
of my car for months. Then one day, I'm at
an old folding table at the local thrift, setting
the crumpled bags next to shoes, an old toaster,
used toys. But the donation slip—how to value
all they represent? I take one last look into
the crumpled bag at the patterns and bright colors
before thickly turning away.

> *This is me now—wild thing returned*
> *to freedom. Sunrise after sunrise, I wake*
> *to this surprise: I, alone, pilot the*
> *day's wide sky. My only job now is to fly.*

First Anniversary of the Last Shift, 9/20/2021

Leaves whirl earthward and a year has passed
since my last shift at the hospital where I worked
from the day it first opened, spring of 1990.
Tectonic, retirement's immediate aftermath,
a chasm I fell into—glee mixed with shock,
mixed with multi-system exhaustion.
I determined to live the seasons as sabbatical:
resetting, reinhabiting, reinventing as everything
scabbed over, thickened to scar.

       Sometimes, I trace the raised flesh—
as if a dream, someone's story I just read about.
       Like *Nurse Nancy,* a Little Golden Book
I read at age eight, with those fancy starred
       and colored band-aids inside. Other times,
I sing the song I scribbled on the back
       of my worksheet that last shift:

I'm breaking ground on a new life,
    giving up all that work strife.
        I let myself begin
            to let myself breathe in . . .

But today, revisiting my nursing poems,
a chemical slurry of stress tornadoes
through my cells: how I tended the sick,
the broken, the dying. The hands I held,
the fights I stood up for—so many days
like working in a war zone, breaking down
my body, my spirit.

How did I do it for thirty-five years, you ask?
It was a calling, a mission—the very earth of me.

Three Years Later

Because every day is Saturday and it's always my weekend off,
and my closet is devoid of nursing uniforms and duty shoes,
my morning starts not to alarm's 5 a.m. explosion, but to sunrise
peeking around the curtains. I shift the low-back ache
as our black cat leaps onto the bed, purring and padding
through my hair fanned across the pillow. I feel the heat
from the man next to me, same heat and same man I've woken to
for more than fifty years. I extricate myself from the chrysalis
of comforter, amble to the bathroom. After, I down a glass
of water to rinse my insides like they say to do, set up
the coffee maker, and check the weather app's forecast. Then,
I look out the kitchen windows to marvel at cloud formations,
the oaks with blue jays bouncing limb to limb, the sometimes deer
wandering through our flower beds. I might decide to brew decaf
and feed the cat. Or instead, go back to bed for one more
snuggle before the day begins its slow unfoldment . . .
its beautiful blossoming.

How to Keep On

Notice the bright moon
kiting over your house
as the sun flares beauty
just the other side of night.
Attend to morning birds,
their determined singing,
no matter what madness
mankind bestows.

Then, drive yourself
to the roadside stand
just outside of town. Choose a flat
of the reddest berries you can find
and pop them into your mouth
whole—with such wild glee
you can't stop long enough
to start the car.

Juice dribbles
down your chin as you embrace
the one thing lovelier
than a strawberry:
the sun-ripe heart
and rhythmic beat
of hope: the radiance and pull
of its insistent flame.

The Heart of the Matter

Because I was born into wonder
        and morning flutters wind and bird song.

Because I have grown children, a life of fruit
        and weeds. Have been a nurse

for the young and the aged and many times
        have closed the eyes of the dead.

I believe with every cell what my hospice patient
        told me: *Love is all there is.*

But some days, I feel like a seed caught
        in layers of drift and eddy, aswirl

in worry's bright heat. When the carousel
        of it all wakes me in the night, I step outside

into starlight spattering the night's inky sea.
        Under those perfect, infinite fires

I cast the magnetic field of my heartbeat outward,
        concentric circles sparking and spinning

in every direction. A body-prayer to every living thing:
        For wellness. For peace. For love.

Afterword

After graduating from Santa Rosa Junior College in California, 1985, I was finally able to sign *R.N.* after my name . . . after years of school with small children, and a husband who commuted three hours a day to work in San Francisco. During those hard times, I'd bolt out of bed at 4:15 a.m., stumble around as the coffee pot filled, while fixing everyone's breakfast and lunch. As soon as the hubby left, I'd grab a steaming mug and study until it was time to get the kids up, dressed, fed and dropped off at Grandma's or school, so I could get to an 8 a.m. class, or an even earlier clinical rotation.

But hospitals weren't hiring new grads then. My first job was in the sub-acute unit of a skilled nursing facility, where I happily earned $10 an hour. The following spring, I accepted a night-shift, on-call position in a local hospital's medical/surgical/orthopedic unit, just as the AIDS epidemic was hitting with full force: a scary and sorrowful time.

And even though it broke my heart over and over, I loved being a nurse. The providing of physical, emotional and spiritual care for patients and their families as they struggled through some of the most difficult times of their lives. Then again in the early 2000s, as the hospital environment changed with the advent of computers and technology, when "high touch" became "high tech." I witnessed the end of an era: hand-written orders, notes and physical charts were replaced by electronic charting. (We were told computer charting would give nurses more time at the bedside. It did not. How can you hold a patient's hand when both of yours are employed at a keyboard?)

As health care became more commodified and industrialized, budgets tightened and the units never seemed to have enough staff. Many days, there was more work than could be physically done in a shift, and we could only provide hurried, basic care. Over the thirty-five years of my career, the population of hospitalized patients grew increasingly sicker: many less critical patients were managed in the emergency department or outpatient settings. At the same time, hospital stays were of shorter and shorter duration. The nurses' daily assignments were marked by a continual stream of discharges followed quickly by admissions of new patients with more complex needs. By the time I retired, a patient receiving a total hip replacement went from an average stay of five days, to going home the same day as their surgery.

Most days, with the rapid turnover, higher patient acuity and increased workloads, the medical/surgical units were noisy, crazy, pressure-cookers of stress. But still, I enjoyed using my expertise to care for my patients, while being the senior nurse and supporting my colleagues. I brought my special interest in holistic care to patients and staff, using my skills as a certified Reiki Master, a Vision Quest Guide, a visual and literary artist. I created the Art at the Bedside project, teaching patients to make collages for stress relief, and to journal as a healing and self-reflective practice. I became a licensed provider of continuing education for registered nurses through the California Board of Registered Nursing, focusing on various aspects of holistic wellness. I was part of a research project using Guided Imagery to assist patients to prepare for surgery, which was successfully implemented across our Northern California hospital system.

I started writing poetry in 1999, and quickly found a place for all the things I witnessed and experienced in life and on the job—it was so very healing and satisfying to make poetic art of it. When I began sharing my poetry, I saw how it moved people, creating a window into the world of hospitals and the nursing profession. My poems seemed to offer hope for a future time when they or a loved one might be hospitalized.

Then another epidemic hit, bookending the final chapter of my work life: the Coronavirus. I retired in September of 2020, nine months after the start. My retirement event, which my daughter and family hosted, consisted of a tailgate party in the hospital parking garage at 3:30 in the afternoon, after my final work shift. What a strange, new land I entered: no important job to do, travel restrictions, isolating at home. Everyone masked and gripped by fear. But somehow, four years have sped by. Life has normalized on many levels and I've finally healed from work trauma. I no longer wake up in a sweaty panic after a nightmare where I'm late for my shift, wearing my uniform inside out and can't log onto the computer—as it gets later and later into the day, meds overdue, call lights blazing and all my patients hollering, *Nurse . . . Nurse!!!*

While there's much I'm glad to have left behind, I miss witnessing the body's miracle and being part of a team of dedicated, amazing people. But most especially, I miss the relationships and soul connection with patients and their families. Of my long, long career, I can truly say I am glad that I answered the call to become an R.N. It was exciting, incredible, difficult, and rewarding—and I would do it again in a proverbial heartbeat.

Peace, blessings, and good health to you and yours,
Shawna L. Swetech, R.N.
October 29, 2024
Forestville, California

About the Author

Shawna L. Swetech lives in Northern California with her husband, a dog, one cat, and nine laying hens. She has two married adult children and two granddaughters. She enjoys hiking in the local forests, sitting by the ocean, travel-trailering, and visiting family in California and North Carolina. She tends a large garden in which she grows vegetables, medicinal herbs, and a wide variety of weeds. Shawna is a mixed-media visual artist and frequently writes ekphrastic poems based on her art work. She is also a wellness coach, utilizing the teachings of Nichiren Buddhism, nature-based spiritual practices, Reiki, nutrition, medicinal herbs, flower essences, art-making, and journaling to assist clients on their healing journeys. She is a co-host for the monthly poetry reading series Rivertown Poets. Shawna believes nature, poetry, and art are important medicines for the ills of our modern world.

www.ingramcontent.com/pod-product-compliance
Lightning Source LLC
Chambersburg PA
CBHW071011160426
43193CB00012B/2004